River, Run!

CAITLIN JACKSON

atmosphere press

River, Run!

Table of Contents

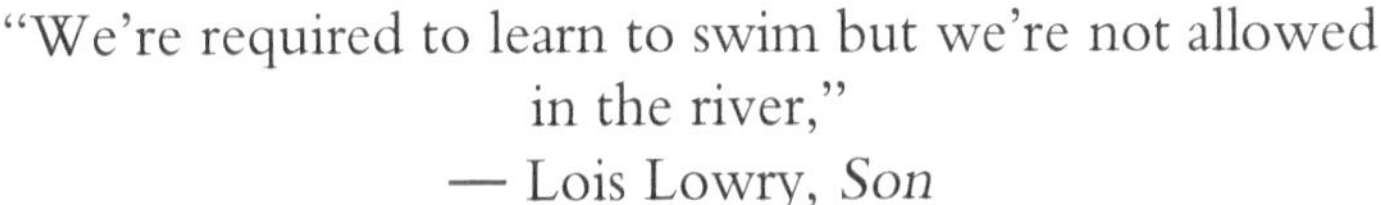

"We're required to learn to swim but we're not allowed in the river,"
— Lois Lowry, *Son*

Secrets

A man came to a village
and ordered all the Women:
bring out your nightclothes!

They emerged with long white gowns
soft robes, waxy thin shirts,
worn pants and glowing swaths
of luminous air. He hung them up
in the town square for everyone to see
and left the next day with a smirk.

The Woman took a robe
to wrap around herself
and on the sleeves she saw
the deep of space
filled with stars
whose end had already come.

Bodies

The village has a river
modest, it runs straight and full of stones.
Far in the distance,
the Woman knows,
there are other waters,
huge and deep.
So vast the moon struggles
to tug them between silver beams.
It is far, but also—
it froths and laps
against her own shores.
Sometimes raging
with crashing waves.

She struggles to keep her head
above water,
fighting to stay afloat.

The Women

who have no children
do not cook or clean.
They hide branches
among the trees
and then lose track of where
they placed them.

They float in the river
and drink
and drink.

It is icy and new
and when they peer
into the surface
they see no reflection.

Baleen

With water running through their teeth like whales,
the Women in the village fish from the stream.
When they catch one, they toss it to shore.
The more they bend to drink, the thicker
their foreheads become. The smaller and redder
their eyes grow.
The Mothers come, bringing their sons who shout
with joy and collect the fish from the soft banks.
They will eat them later
with glasses full of cold milk
for their growing bones.
The Women keep drinking and tossing
the fish they will not eat. Their teeth become longer
and thinner. Their arms grow shorter and wider.
The Mothers smile and thank them but do not meet
their now tiny eyes.
They take the small sticky hands of their children,
and the silver scaled twisting fish,
and they walk back to the village
maybe telling a story
or singing a song.
The Women still drink. At least the water
is cold and clean, and the mothers' singing
sometimes floats on the breeze
back for them to hear.

Sometimes it stays in the air for hours.

Wild

The Mothers hold their children.
The Women's hands are empty.
The Mothers sing a lullaby, soft
and sweet. The Women sing
a different song. Fierce and full
of howls beneath
dark branches reaching
like open arms
to cradle the Women
until they finally lose their voices.

Fest

In the middle of the village, there is a pole.
The Boys and Girls gather round in the spring
to dance and wrap it in bright colors.
The Mothers watch closely,
the Women keep their distance.
The Boys tug the Girls' hair like taffy.
It grows and coils around the pole,
which, strung now in gold,
glimmers in the sun.

Next year the colors will be the same
but the faces will be older. The Mothers
mourn the change.
The Women stand still, eager,
waiting from their distance.

Wave

The Woman's hand was disappearing
first bits of nail, then strips
of flesh then whole knuckle bones—
drifting away. When she held it in the air
the wind caught fragments
that waved like laundry on the line
or a battle flag.

One afternoon, she went to the river.
She waded into the water, it was clear
to the bottom so when she bent
and dipped her hand in
she could see the fish come
and fight over the skin
blossoming in the current—

until nothing was left
but water flowing.

Bide

The Woman has stopped drinking from the river.
Now her hours have slowed.
She watches time pass with beats
in between her heart's.
She feels her skin begin to peel
down to something else—
silver scales, a long lashing tail
split down the middle.
Her bones begin to seep out of her body.
She saves them carefully, hides them
where the Man will not find them.

Each morning she goes to the river.
She puts her feet in and watches.

Wool

The fields are full of sheep.
Belly down, the dogs crawl
to keep them in check.
The Man guides his friends
with whistles and clicks.
Cetacean–like,
they swim together on dry land.

The Woman stays at home, waiting.
She is always thirsty.

Galaxies

I.

The Woman breaks her mirror.
She wants to slice herself with the glass,
enjoy the rich red of her blood.
Instead, she can only stare
and, in pieces,
look back.

II.

The Woman is thirsty. She wants to drink.
The river is guarded, and her well water
has become brackish
and turns black as she pours it.
Her throat stays dry.

III.

The Woman counts the cobblestones.
She counts pebbles she scoops from the side of the
square.
She lines them up in no order,
she promised to stop
but it continues day and night.

There is no peace and the stars are angry in the sky.

Echoes

At night the village whispers, it throbs.
Boys flit bat-like across the square
they carry messages the Women cannot read.

The Women lie in bed, lids pressed down, windows
shut tight. They can feel the secrets swarm—
an insect cloud that circles the moon.

The Girls toss in their beds, asleep,
but not deeply. They are becoming.

What is to be done?

The Women will get no rest, the square shudders
in the dark. The Boys scoop the swarms
into their beaked mouths. They chirp higher
than the Women can hear.
Still, in dreams or awake, the Women know
the secrets,
and their stomachs curdle with them.

Glamour

The Woman drinks again
in her dreams
it is daytime and sunlight
pours golden syrup
onto green leaves outside her window.
The world is pausing,
and she can finally breathe,
joy swells.

When she wakes she goes to the river
the morning sun shines dapples
onto its bed, inviting.
She walks, then runs—
the stones
bruising her heels,
cutting her toes.

Still, she almost makes it to the trees,
before her legs buckle
and the current takes her.

Type

The Man twitches in his sleep.
The Woman smells him, his back
facing her, solid and unmoving.

The river is always moving.
I'll go fish, the Man says,
and he does.

The Woman rolls out dough
on a dry surface—
she sprinkles it full of flour.

What mystery will we solve tonight?
She asks.
No mystery for us.
He says.
We just have to wait.
He answers and answers
but she cannot wait.
She is not that type.

Flock

During the day there's stomach ache
and nights are full of black wings
beating beating.
And beaks full of sharp teeth
that clack when they snap shut.

The Woman does not know how to drive them away.
She shoots into the air but they do not scatter.
She screams and waves her arms
but they flock closer
until the world has shrunk
to black feathers and beady eyes.

Witch

Even in her dreams, now,
she does not drink from the river.
Instead, she practices secret magic.
She shouts in tongues and levitates,
power streaming
from her fingers.

Behind, the mob comes with their torches
their pitchforks, she casts her glance
back to the square and braces herself.

Wolves

The villagers whisper
in the forest *there might be wolves.*
There are signs—
a muddy footprint,
a glint of white fang
beneath the moon.
The Mothers lock their doors,
the Men growl into the night.

The Women stride into the forest—
hair blowing, arms outstretched
a strange and wild song
filling the air around them.

Et Sorores

Outside the village
in the woods, there is a pool
where the Women go to swim.
They can talk here since,
deep in the trees, their words get caught
and garbled before they reach the sky
and so their meaning will not spread.
The exclamations pause, then bounce
back to the Women's ears echoing
down through the boughs
like cathedral song pivoting to earth.
The Women paddle quietly,
cold black depths above
and below, the air thick with words
pealing with the joy of bells.

Flight

I.

The Women are of the type
that do not scream or jump
as hornets, delicate jewel bodies
glittering full of afternoon sun,
crawl along their skin.

They brush them off,
one after the other,
and watch them fly away.

II.

The Women gather—
some of them have been coming
to this clearing
a long time.
Some of them arrive now fresh
and scared,
but as they listen the leaves
above their heads,
the clouds in the sky
and a distant bird
all call to them.

They are ready to taste the wind
as they learn to fly now
together.

Precipitation

Some days the village leans sideways.
Then the people step carefully
so as not to slide off.
For the Woman, the ground is
always slippery, unsafe.

On the tilted days her feet sweep
from under her, pushed over edge
like water rushing over falls.

She longs for deep fresh snow,
to brace herself in a still clean morning.
A bird rustles on a nearby branch.
She holds her breath, waiting
for the thud of wings
as he rises.

Quakes

The Mothers gather to whisper
and point with their chins
while their eyes roll to the sky.

The Women shift their feet one
to the other, the ground is uneasy
beneath them.

At night they dream the land rises,
bucks up into hills then higher still
until it towers to the sky.

Even in dreams though,
the mountains are distant
and they cannot leave the village.

After all
there is work to be done
while whisper words swirl above
and the earth shifts below.

Tales

The Women teach the children to swim
while the Mothers watch.
Boys and Girls paddle in the river
and cast anxious glances at the dark green
of the trees that line the horizon.

One day, some of the Girls may venture among them
count the leaves and smell the earth
until a pool rises before them,
clear and cold and a secret whispered.

The Women teach these ones about mermaids,
about sirens.
They teach them how to sing.

Twitch

The Man chops wood.
His axe is heavy, but he does not falter.
The Boys watch open mouthed.
The Girls watch the Boys watching.
They will not chop the wood,
but they will use it to fuel their fires
and make their pots bubble.

A squirrel sits in a nearby tree.
He rattles, he hesitates,
then he scampers closer.
He watches the axe rise and fall,
his tail twitches. He knows
there will come a time
when the Man lets his hands,
slick with sweat and grime
slip.

Queen

The Woman writhes in pain. In her snakes
coil in wrathful slumber, their shining
scales slither around and around
the inside of her throat.
Outside—
only sighs escape,
a wind long lost among the trees.

Back in the river, when she was safe,
she'd float to the sky, relaxing
into clouds'
billowing embrace, water droplets
forming along her brow like jewels.

Those days are past though.
The snakes are always
waiting to strike.

If only she could feel the prick
of their fangs
and know it was over at last.

Crowned

The Man wrinkles his nose at the children,
the Girls and the Boys.
He shies away from blossoming bellies
and mewling cries for milk.

Instead, he thinks of the sea
and the smell the air holds there.
A salt that flavors each hour
and never washes away.
A dolphin might jump, beady eyes
shining in the sunlight.
He lowers his hand to her brow.

The Woman remembers what it was like
to leap in the waves
before she was touched.

Panic

The Women hate to be alone.
And they hate to be with the people.
On rainy days they revel in water's company
as drops hit their upturned faces.
On sunny days they can plant their feet
firmly into the river and feel the song
of the current and the stones.

But on dark days there is only silence
and the land is dry as their angry bones.

Surrender

The Woman stops swimming
and lets the river take her,
when she tries to stand
the sharp stones cut her feet.

So she floats,
and the trees are dark on the horizon.

Run-on

The river has begun to run
from the Woman's eyes
and mouth.
She cannot make it stop.
She is full of smooth worn pebbles.
They push at her eyes from the inside
and fish flip against her tongue.

She is suddenly in the square,
water pouring out onto the stones.
She mouths for help as it laps against her teeth.

The people come to watch. They see her retreat,
the flow finally staunching.
They think nothing much of it.

Din

The village used to leave the Woman alone.
By herself, frantic thuds and clicks
would echo in her ears.
The pounding of feet on the earth,
the rapping of nails on a table,
a muscle tensing in her jaw...
But in her right mind, the noise
would turn to music and her air
became thick with song.

Now they corner her,
push her in locked rooms and bore
into her with their eyes.
In her ears there is only clatter.
And maybe, her voice was always broken,
but at least before she wanted to sing.

Ballad

The wolves have not seen the Woman
in many days.
She has been locked away,
her voice removed.
Forbidden to swim in the river
or enter the forest
and play as she used to
with pricked ears
and tails wagging
and the sky filled with
their mingling howls.

The howls now have a different sound—
alone, the wolves' music is not the same.

Wish

The Woman cannot leave.

She watches the village ebb
and flow outside the window.
The tide tugs at her.

She dreams of the ocean
of diving birds and deep
black waters, of salty wind
that lifts her to her toes.

Hunger

The Woman has lost her appetite.
Every night she dreams of the cobblestone square.
She thinks she'll die there.
They'll gather someday,
to pin her to the sky and watch
as she catches starlight like fire.

Every day where she walks a trail of leaves
lingers behind, fading from green
into dry brown pieces.

And she bakes her loaves diligently,
the bread sticks in her throat.

Droplets

The Woman hears the raindrops
outside early in the morning.
She thinks of drinking the water
from the sky, of lapping it from
puddles and blades of grass.

She watches the stars on a clear night
and prays for rain.

Drowned

The Woman hasn't gone to the river
but the water is already in her lungs.
The Mothers and Children stand by
and watch her gasp for air.

Outside the river swells
as it begins to rain.

Dry

The Woman is thirsty—
she is parched.
All she wants is water
cold so it hurts her teeth,
or hot to burn her inside.
She'll lie down in the river
and the current will flow down her throat.
If the whole ocean poured in,
it would not be enough.

She asks for nothing but to drink until the world ends.

Air

The Women pull the cover of night over their heads.
They breathe like they were taught,
in
then out
then in
and hold it.
Those long moments, filled with air,
but no breath, remind them of death.

The next day the Boys play in the field,
the Girls run to their Mothers
and whisper secrets they learned watching legs churn
and kick and run.

The Women stand and wait for night to come again.

Stone

The Woman used to shriek, and squawk.
She'd raise her arms as wings and flap
around the village. Some would stare, but others
would join in and caw and flap along
and, though hoarse,
 it could be a joyous sound.

But now the Woman will not raise her arms
or make the noise of birds.
No one will join her, and
she must be still
and small and quiet.
A stone, a pebble even,
in the bed of the river.
She must not stir, or the waters' flow
will be disturbed.

And when she stays
still and small,
she is safe.
She will be safe.

Undressed

The Women begin to peel away their skin
They pop out their eyes and gently
remove all their bones.

The Mothers are too busy
to stop them.
The Man has faded away.

The Women are covered now,
their scales glitter in moonlight.
They're diving in.

End-Scene

The Woman wades into the river.
The water is cold on her toes,
lapping against her shins
her scales
her fins.
Her mouth opens
closes against the air.
She flicks her splitting tail.

Now she will fall to her knees
and we zoom out
to see the sky, gray and open-armed
and the village lying below
in wait.

Tick-Tock

The Man chips away at his toes, his knees
his jawline. He carefully constructs
what he calls the perfect machine.
It sits, full of careful beauty
waiting to rip him in four parts.

The Woman wrings her hands
she wiggles her toes in the cold river,
her flesh becomes clammy, unwanted
it turns to slough.

The Man sits in his corner, mumbling
he hammers away at his knuckles,
his fingernails, his fine eyelashes.
They fall to the floor.
He is taking himself apart
The Woman longs to swim away
while behind her,
everything comes back together.

Silver

The Man is made of metal.

On his slick surface is the reflection
 of rushing water, far off trees
and the bridge
of the Woman's nose.

The Woman's toes are icy
from the river.
When she shifts in bed
the Man moves away.

Voyages

The Man and the Woman
separate.

The Man's hands turn to clockwork
clacking and whining until
he rubs them with oil.
Once they smoothly run again,
he measures out the air with tiny spoons
and, when he is done,
 releases it back to into the sky.

It returns to its journey to distant stars.

The Woman dreams of the ocean,
waves breaking at her toes,
swirls of light against the dark.
She has galaxies beneath her eyelids
if only the Man knew
he might stay home.

Wisp

Some Girls have learned to step
into the thin of air.
The Boys do not even come to watch
they occupy themselves on distant hills
with matters they consider vast.
They study earth and grass and sky
down to every blade and speck of dirt.

The Girls rise up and soar.
They taste the clouds and sun,
they stretch their arms and fingers,
and starlight shines down their open throats
as they start to sing.

Hope

The Man would like to captain a ship.
The Woman wants to run away.
They'd like to sail into every sunset
that comes next.

The Woman asks when they can leave.
The Man holds his hands up to the sky
he sees through them to the stars
he takes their bearings.

They build the ship of bone,
it floats nonetheless.

Finale

It was cold the morning
the Woman went to the river for the last time.

The Man loves to fix watches
when he can find the time.
He fits the pieces together
with his clever fingers
and listens for their soft
ticking heartbeats.

As she made her way,
the Woman felt the chilled dew on her feet
and the wind licked at her face.

The Man was asleep,
listening
for a sound that would not come.

Ritual

Streams of skin blow across the village.
It is not clear
whose they are.
The people search and search
and finally, underneath a far hill
they find a stack of bones..
One by one,
they toss them into the river.

Acknowledgments

"Baleen" previously appeared in *The Halcyone Magazine*.

"Et Sorores" previously appeared in *Cathexis Northwest Press*, October 1, 2019.

About Atmosphere Press

Atmosphere Press is an independent, full-service publisher for excellent books in all genres and for all audiences. Learn more about what we do at atmospherepress.com.

We encourage you to check out some of Atmosphere's latest releases, which are available at Amazon.com and via order from your local bookstore:

A Synonym for Home, poetry by Kimberly Jarchow
The Cry of Being Born, poetry by Carol Mariano
Big Man Small Europe, poetry by Tristan Niskanen
In the Cloakroom of Proper Musings, a lyric narrative by Kristina Moriconi
Lucid_Malware.zip, poetry by Dylan Sonderman
The Unordering of Days, poetry by Jessica Palmer
It's Not About You, poetry by Daniel Casey
A Dream of Wide Water, poetry by Sharon Whitehill
Radical Dances of the Ferocious Kind, poetry by Tina Tru
The Woods Hold Us, poetry by Makani Speier-Brito
My Cemetery Friends: A Garden of Encounters at Mount Saint Mary in Queens, New York, nonfiction and poetry by Vincent J. Tomeo
Report from the Sea of Moisture, poetry by Stuart Jay Silverman
The Enemy of Everything, poetry by Michael Jones
The Stargazers, poetry by James McKee
The Pretend Life, poetry by Michelle Brooks
Minnesota and Other Poems, poetry by Daniel N. Nelson

About the Author

Caitlin Jackson is a poet. She graduated from Oberlin College and has an MFA from University of Central Florida. She lives in Florida with her partner and elderly terrier mix. She is always scouring the real world for telltale signs of the epic and mythical. This is her second full length book of poetry. Her first collection, *Myths for Small Matters*, was published in December 2016.

www.ingramcontent.com/pod-product-compliance
Lightning Source LLC
LaVergne TN
LVHW050423160726
843469LV00041B/1207